"Life will be **ok!**"

THE ABC'S OF OCD

WRITTEN AND ILLUSTRATED
BY KATHLEEN DUNN, AGE EIGHT

Published by

The **CREATIVE** CABIN

PITTSBURGH, PA

COPYRIGHT ©2010

ALL RIGHTS RESERVED
INCLUDING THE RIGHT OF REPRODUCTION
IN WHOLE OR IN PART IN ANY FORM.

Printed in the USA
ISBN 978-1-60725-809-4

www.abcocd.com

"Throughout my years in private practice, I have always believed that
the greatest source of wisdom comes from the people we serve.
This is especially true of our youngest patients, who often see their life situations clearly,
and without the filters of theory, statistics or diagnostic guidelines.

The insight, humor and warmth of this book is an example of the best resources of the human spirit!
Healing comes in many forms and Kathleen Dunn has captured the essence of a difficult disorder
that has affected but not defeated her family. It is a tribute to the entire Dunn family that they have chosen
to devote their creative energy to provide this beautiful book to educate others.

To me "The ABC's of OCD spell h-o-p-e!"

Dr. Mary M. Brand, Ph.D. Psychologist, Alliance Psychological Services, LLC

"Humor, perseverance, and family support are qualities that Kathleen
and her family brought with them to therapy. One step at a time Kathleen learned how
to "Boss Back OCD" and understand Obsessive Compulsive Disorder in a new way.

May others learn from you, Kathleen.

Thank you for sharing your experience through the "ABC's".

Dr. Miriam DeRiso, Ph.D. Licensed Psychologist

"I LOVE IT!

I can really relate to it. I like the way it's illustrated, and the
cute sense of humor in there really strikes a chord in me with my
son. Anyone with an OCD child is going to read **The ABC's of OCD** over
and over again. Tell Kathleen I think she's outstanding!"

Parent, K. H., Master Personal Fitness Trainer

KATHLEEN'S STORY

Hi, my name is Kathleen, I am nine years old and I have Obsessive Compulsive Disorder.
My mom figured out I had OCD when I was six, she knew what was happening since my older sister Bridget also has it. When I was six I had a lot of weird habits. Some of them I don't even like to talk about now. The main habit, that I don't mind telling you about was that I would say 'I think' before everything I said! I mean everything. At first it seemed funny but then I couldn't stop saying it no matter what. I also did a lot of checking, like the bathroom and lights and doors. I would worry about all of these things ~ all the time. Many times I would have to sit with my mom at night on the couch and try to stop my mind from racing about my worries.

My mom found a really nice doctor that helps other kids with OCD and we started to meet at her office in town. She showed me ways to start to boss back my worries. We even named the 'worry' a funny name so that when I had it, I could say the funny name to take my mind off of it. After practicing this a lot, my worries would go away.

Another thing I love to do to keep my mind off of my worries is write and draw and do art. When I was eight I wrote this book with the letters of the alphabet about my OCD. I really liked working on something and my mom said this might be able to help other kids with OCD. When I do my writing and art I don't worry about things so much. My mom helped me put my words and my picture of my 'Boss Back' person on the computer so we could make a book. We named him 'BossBax' and I made a big group of them so we added them all to this book.

I like glow-in-the-dark so we have that on the edges of the book to make it more fun to have.

Now that I am nine, my OCD has gotten much better. I am very glad that I went to the OCD doctor to learn how to tell my habits to go away. Sometimes they are still there but the habits don't bother me as much. I like to say 'Life will be OK', that's in my book too!

FOREWARD BY TEENAGE SISTER

Hi, my name is Bridget, Kathleen's 17 year old sister.

We share our bedroom, where I keep my clothes and make-up completely neat. If Kathleen moves my clothes or touches anything I get mad because it makes me really uncomfortable and my OCD really bothers me. (I keep checking all of it!) We made Kathleen a spot in the hall for her clothes and she has a 'loft' for toys. Sometimes at night we send notes up and down the bunk beds and talk about our OCD. It is nice to have 'company' with it.

When I found out that my little sister also had OCD, I was not too concerned, because I would know how to help her get through it. Even though it gets tough at times, I realize that everybody has something they have to deal with. My sister and I make the best of it, just so she doesn't touch my closet and make-up!

A

is for **Always**

doing it

AGAIN!

I hope I get this right or I'll have to do it again.

A is also for Anxiety, which is another name for worries.
It is best not to Avoid your OCD.
Do not run Away from it, beating the OCD tricks is All About
facing them and Attacking back!

B

is for

you can get

BETTER

from your OCD!

B is also for Bossing Back your OCD Bothers.
Believe me, even Breathing long and slow Breaths
is very helpful with the Bossing Back.

C

I still **CAN**

play !

when I have OCD

oh, yes <u>you</u> Can!

C is also part of CBT which means Cognitive Behavioral Therapy.
This is the best way to treat OCD if you need some help with it.

There are **Different** kinds of OCD

E

Elephants

could have some OCD.

!

E is also for Eating right Each day ~ good food helps you feel Extremely great too!

F

OCD is not always **Fair**
but you can have **Fun** with it
and give your OCD
a **Funny** name!

I am king
of the mountain

G

it is **GOOD**

to have people help you with it.
Getting together with others
in a **Group** is a **Great**
way to beat your OCD!

H

My mom is *always* **Happy** *to* **Help** me **Help** myself with my OCD **habits!**

There are many other people who can Help you learn to Help yourself!

Do you like my pink hair? I think I do!

"think"

my book will help you

smile at your OCD •

(saying **I think** *was one of my 'habits')*

I is also for Irritated.
This is a big word for when you feel like you have too much energy.
If you practice, Inch~by~Inch, your OCD worries can go away!

J

You can do a

JIG

after your ocd goes to sleep.

(JUMP around and Just have fun!)

J is also for the Junky thoughts you might have with your OCD.
Just throw them away out of your head while you Jump rope and have fun!

K

My name is **Kathleen** and I have OCD.

My mom is **Kate** and she loves me the way I am!

K is for all of the Kind people that can help you!

L

Lollipops

might help too!

L is also for Limit.
Give your OCD habit a Limit.
Maybe check your Lunch twice instead
of three times today.
Don't Let OCD go over the Limit.
Tomorrow you may be Lucky enough
to check on your Lunch only once!

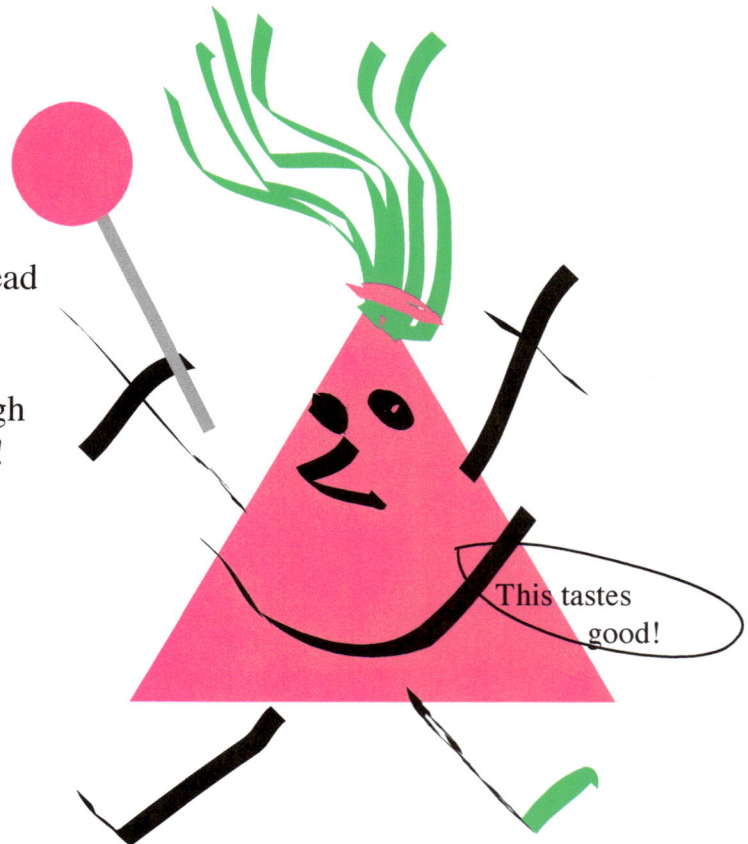

This tastes good!

M

Sometimes **Medicine**

might help you too…

My sister takes hers when

my mom

re**m**inds her! **Me** too!

(I don't **mind** at all that I do not take **medicine.**)

N

Never

think that you cannot have fun with OCD ...

YOU CA**N**! Just give your OCD habit a funny

Nickname and it will be easier to

tell it to go away!

You will feel **Noticeably Normal** again!

O

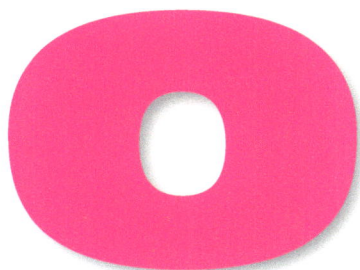

is for OBSESSIVE

which means wanting to

keep doing 'it' again.

Oh my, you have to learn to not listen to this O!

push this ! away!

O is also for Opposite. This may take practice but Over time it really helps you.
Do the Opposite of what your OCD tells you to do.
Rather than avoid a doorknob, just grab hold Of it!

P

ALL types of
People

can help you with OCD.

P is also for thoughts that Pop into your mind
and make you feel anxious or uncomfortable.
When you learn to Push these away by Playing,
your OCD will go away.

Q

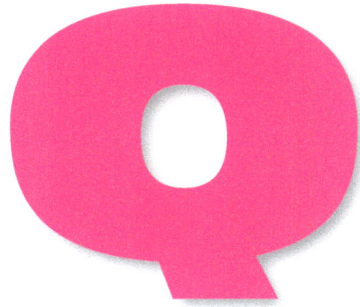

You cannot just **quit** this OCD,

you have to practice

quitting!

The more you practice **quitting** funny

OCD **Quirks** will **Quickly** go away!

R

OCD

can be **Really** hard.

<u>REMEMBER</u>

you **really** might just outgrow it.

R is also for Ritual.
Tell OCD 'You are not my boss!'
Change your Routine and do your Ritual your own way.
Do it different each time! Then you are Really in charge!

S

On **Somedays**

your

OCD **S**eems to

away.

SUDDENLY SLIP

Playing outSide and Sports for exercise is a Splendid idea to help OCD Slip away!

Standing on one foot takes your mind off of OCD.

You have **To Tell** yourself

The liTTle TRICKS to

remember **t**hat you **can** do i**t**.

and Talk back to your OCD … a little Therapy may even go a long way!

U

Go **under**

your bed to hide from your OCD.

Play tent to get your mind off of it,

under there!

U is also for Understanding OCD
so you can know when a worry is OCD,
and tell it to "go away!"

V

I am **Very**

good at getting away from my OCD.
The more you practice the easier it is, you can be
VICTORIOUS over OCD!

W

If your dog is **wagging** his tail he got rid of his OCD ...

or he is counting the

wags!

W is also for Winning!
You Win When **you** decide What to do,
do not let the OCD decide.

X

You do not need

xrays

to prove you have OCD!

X is for putting a big X mark on OCD,

"I'm not listening to you, OCD!"

You do not have control over me!

y

If

YOU

have some OCD

YOU

should stop worr**y**ing ...

z

At least you are not a
zebra

trying to keep his

zigzags

straight all day!

THE END!

About OCD, Obsessive Compulsive Disorder

Parents may begin to notice that their child is telling them they are having thoughts that are "weird", or that they can't get certain images out of their head. A child may begin to engage in repeated handwashing or avoidance of touching certain objects to cope with a fear of germs. A child may begin to express high amounts of doubt about whether they are saying something true, which is clearly true, like, "my favorite color is blue". The child with Obsessive Compulsive Disorder (OCD) may also worry that if they do not say a word or do a certain set of behaviors that harm might come to someone they love. These irrational thoughts are called obsessions, and the actions children perform to try to relieve the anxiety associated with the obsessions are called compulsions.

Many children hide their obsessions and compulsions because they feel embarrassed, or out-of-control. Parents may not understand how or why their child developed these new fears. Current research suggests that OCD is inherited. In other words, there are usually other family members in the child's family tree that have OCD. The research indicates that people with OCD may have a difference in the amount of serotonin that is found in the brain. For this reason sometimes medication that influences serotonin can be helpful in relieving OCD symptoms. A psychiatrist can be helpful in identifying whether your child is a good candidate for medication. Another way to address OCD is with Cognitive Behavioral Therapy (CBT). These techniques are very helpful for teaching children tools to "talk back" to their OCD.

Step One
Identify "worries" as OCD, not you. Some children even give their OCD a name like "Boogie Man", or "habits", or "worry-bug". The idea of naming the OCD, or referring to it as separate from the person, is to empower the child to fight back. Letting a child know that the parents and therapist are also on the child's "team" to help win against OCD, can also be helpful. Other ways to empower the child can be helping the child imagine themselves as a superhero, and the OCD as tiny.

Step Two
"Bossing Back" OCD is a technique, first described by John March, M.D. Bossing Back OCD involves helping the child develop a way to answer their OCD thoughts, like "I don't have to listen to you, worry-bug, go away!", "Leave me alone, Boogie Man thoughts!". Kids can also be encouraged to tell the truth to their OCD, like "My mother is a good driver, and she has never been in a car crash, so I'm not going to listen to you!"

Step Three
Distraction, or getting off the OCD "track" is a very important technique for children to learn as they start to understand and master their OCD. Children and parents can work together to identify what types of activities are helpful for "distraction". The activity needs to be highly absorbing, such as playing with an electronic game, watching a movie, or playing with a friend or pet. A less absorbing activity such as reading or watching television, sometimes still allows space for the OCD thoughts to continue.

Step Four
Exposure and Response Prevention is the CBT technique of gradually facing the feared activity, engaging in it, and then not using a compulsion. For example, some children worry about making a mistake when they are completing a written assignment. So, they may erase and redo, and erase and redo, repeatedly. "Response Prevention" would mean that the child would, at first, only redo one time, and eventually learn to not redo at all. There are various ways to help make exposure and response prevention easier. One, is to go slowly, only gradually reducing the frequency of a response, another is to use distraction, and a third is to use humor. For example, one child had to have her hair part done perfectly, so in humor she would mess her hair up to look really funny, and then walk around the house that way. She would laugh, and so would everyone else. She called it making fun of OCD.

What does the future hold for a child with OCD?
One way to think of the CBT coping techniques is to think of them as "tools in a toolbox". Once children learn these techniques they always have them. Periodically, a child's OCD may worsen again, especially during times of stress. If this happens it can be important to practice strategies that have been helpful in the past, and return to see a therapist if needed. These later sessions are called "booster" sessions, and usually a few "booster" sessions help a child remember ways to beat the OCD, or to invent new ones. Once a child and family understand OCD it easier to recognize, identify, and work together to "boss it back".

From Kathleen's therapist, Dr. Miriam DeRiso, Ph.D. Licensed Psychologist

*My*WISH

Dedicated to all families who deal with
mental health issues on a daily basis.
My hope is that you and your child
find warm humor in these pages.
While Obsessive Compulsive Disorder,
or any mental health challenge, can be
very frustrating for both you and your child,
maintaining a sense of calm to cope
with the challenges of daily
life help keep things in perspective.
When you look down the path
you and your child travel, you gather
the courage and fortitude it requires
to continue on with your journey.

Love your child for who they are and will
become. Keep the faith, your sense of humor
and have courage to move forward to enjoy
the blessings each day brings.

Kate Dunn, *Mother*

ACKNOWLEDGEMENTS:
We would like to thank our 'Frank Pap', 1941 ~ 2008, for his 'investment' of a new color
printer for our project and the very first book comps, Author and Friend, Joyce Faulkner,
Writer and Marketing Friend, Autumn Edmiston, and Printer and Friend, Matt Bryer for
helping to keep mom's momentum on track through our 'busy' 08 summer!

Kathleen & Bridget

Kathleen and Bridget dedicate this book to their 'farm pap',
whom we are sure had OCD himself.
His tools were never hung up straight enough,
the grass was always mowed in the 'right' direction,
he counted raspberries to one hundred then started again,
and he counted his steps when he took us for walks!

Our times together and the memories we shared are special ~ as was he.

(1929 ~ 2008)

Printed in the United States
ISBN 978-1-60725-809-4

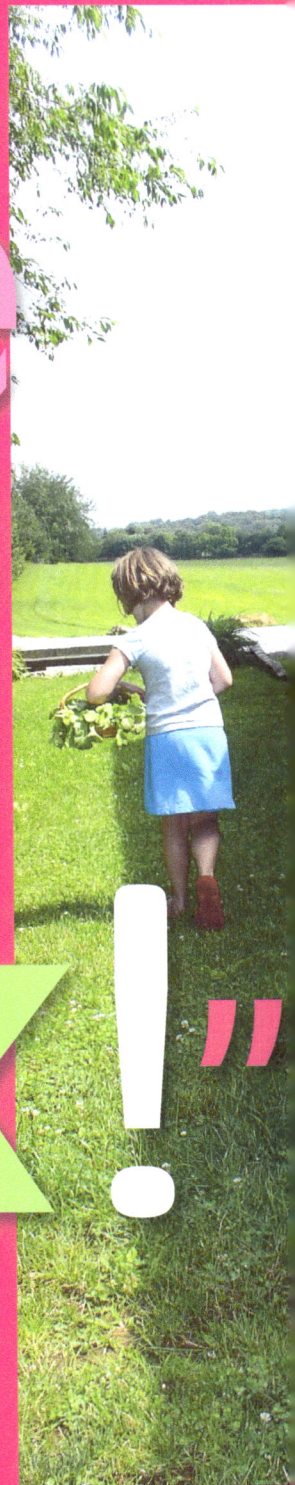

"Life will be **OK!**"

www.ingramcontent.com/pod-product-compliance
Lightning Source LLC
Chambersburg PA
CBHW060815090426
42737CB00002B/67